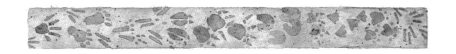

The
Two-Legged
Creature

The Two-Legged Creature

An Otoe Story

Retold by Anna Lee Walters
Illustrated by Carol Bowles

NORTHLAND PUBLISHING

First Edition
ISBN 0-87358-553-4
Library of Congress Catalog Card Number 92-56510

Cataloging-in-Publication Data
Walters, Anna Lee, 1946–
The two-legged creature : an Otoe story / retold by Anna Lee Walters
illustrated by Carol Bowles. — 1st ed.
32 p.   cm.
Summary: This Otoe Indian legend explains how, after a magically harmonious period in the world when Man and the animals lived in peace, Man changed and became abusive, so that only Dog and Horse have remained close.
ISBN 0-87358-553-4 : $14.95
1. Oto Indians—Legends. 2. Animals—Folklore—Juvenile literature. [1. Oto Indians—Legends. 2. Indians of North America—Legends. 3. Man—Influence on nature—Folklore.]
I. Bowles, Carol, ill. II. Title
E99.087W343 1993
398.2'089975—dc20   92-56510

Cover Design by David Jenney
Designed by Rudy J. Ramos

Manufactured in Hong Kong
by Wing King Tong

5-93/7.5M/0426

To C.B., Crystal, Tina and Darren.

—A.L.W.

My people are from the woodlands and prairies. They say the world we live in today was not always the way it is now. There was a very different way of life before the cities were here. The world was magical back then.

Once upon a time, the world was ruled by creatures—animals, insects, birds, and fish of every kind—and they lived together in peace and happiness without argument and fear. With these creatures lived a two-legged one we now call Man, and all the other creatures showed him how to live. There were no towns or houses anywhere.

There were no bicycles or cars. Because there was only one man at the time, the earth was very clean and the sky was very clear.

What was magical about this time was that all the animals, insects, birds, fish, and the two-legged creature spoke one language that they all understood. They spoke in a friendly way to one another. They called each other Brother. For a long time, they lived peacefully with one another.

Each animal, insect, bird, and fish had another name besides Brother, and each one had a special place in the world back then. There were Bear, Fox, Beetle, Termite, Bluebird, Robin, and many others. Man was called the two-legged creature. All of these creatures lived close together then, sharing the earth and sky with one another.

Back then Man was much like the other creatures living on the earth. He lived in the ground like an insect, ate leaves and plants like most of the animals, and climbed trees to gaze at the birds. Man learned how to live by watching the animals, insects, birds, and fish. They taught him everything he knew. But after a while, Man began to act differently from those around him.

One morning, he woke up and crawled out of his home in the ground. Snow lay all around and it shined into his eyes. He brushed out the bright light and saw Bear go by. "Where are you going, Brother?" Man asked.

"Fishing," answered Bear.

"May I go along?" Man asked.

"If you wish, Brother," agreed Bear.

He followed after Bear in the deep snow. The lake was spotted with ice, and the water was freezing cold. Dark little birds played in the water. They dived into it and soared off into the sky again, untouched by the cold.

"Now please be careful, Brother," advised Bear to Man. "You have no fur to protect you from the cold as I have. You do not even have the oily feathers of those little birds playing over there. Bears and birds do not freeze, but you are different."

Man didn't listen. He wanted to play in the water like the birds were doing. Bear stepped into the deep water and shivered. Behind him he heard a great splash! Man lay shivering in the icy water. His face was blue and his teeth chattered loudly.

"I told you, Brother!" said Bear. "Now look at what you have done!"

Bear pulled Man out of the icy water, and all the birds helped pull him to shore, tugging on his buckskin clothing with their tiny sharp beaks. On the shore, Bear dried Man and tried to warm him with his fur.

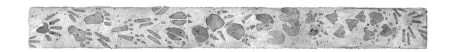

After that, Bear wanted nothing more to do with Man. "He doesn't listen to us any longer," Bear said angrily.

The other animals were now feeling the same way toward Man because he had started to act very differently toward them. One time he said to Skunk, "My, Brother Skunk! How you stink!" Now Skunk had been thinking to himself for some time that Man stunk very badly too, and all the other animals had to agree with Skunk. Skunk had never said this, though, because he was polite and well mannered. But in answer to Man's unkind words, Skunk said, "My Brother! That is exactly what I was thinking about you! You have a very strange odor!"

Besides becoming impolite and unruly, Man always
whined and cried when something did not go his way. None
of the animals did that—it was so disgraceful! Tears welled
up in Man's eyes all the time over every little ache and pain
or when one of the animals, insects, birds, or fish said "no"
to him. They all began to scurry away when Man came
around because he acted this way.

Man started to become mean to the animals, birds, insects, and fish. Whenever he could, he killed spiders with one swipe of his hand, and he happily squashed insects under his big clumsy feet. He began to toss pebbles and rocks at birds and fish. He kicked at Fox and others, sometimes killing them, too. None of the creatures could stand this awful behavior any longer.

"Enough of him!" they said. "We can no longer call him Brother! It was bad enough when he stopped listening to us. Now he is beginning to act as if he is the only one who lives in this world. He has become too destructive! He acts as if he wants to kill all of us!"

They called a meeting to discuss Man's behavior. At the meeting, Bear growled, "Man is destroying all of us in sight!"

Skunk stood up and said, "He stinks real bad, too!"

A tiny black bird stood and paced before the group on stick legs, saying, "He's really not very bright, you know. He is silly enough to freeze if he falls into icy water or is out in a storm alone. All of us are able to survive in any weather, but not he! He's stupid, stupid!"

"Oh, he whines and cries all the time," said a beautiful gray deer. "Animals behave so much better than that!"

All agreed they didn't want Man to mingle with them any longer.

carol Bowles ©1992

CarolBowles © 1992

The meeting lasted for several days and nights because
the animals could not agree on what to do with Man.

"He should live by himself!" said Beaver.

"No, no, he would only die," Elk said. "Though he would
kill us, he is still our brother and we do not wish him death."

Finally, to bring the meeting to a close, Dog stood up
and cleared his throat. "You are all tired of this. I'll go with
Man," he said. "I'll try to keep him from bothering the rest of
you. I'll try to keep him out of trouble. I'll stay by his side."

Then Horse stood, neighed, and pawed the earth. Horse said, "Dog and I come from the same family. He and I belong together. Because he is my little brother, I, too, will go with Man. We will keep him company and be his friend."

The other animals, birds, and insects sighed in great relief.

This is how the two-legged creature separated from all the others and why dogs and horses are so close to people today.

carolBowles © 1992

Of Pawnee-Otoe descent, ANNA LEE WALTERS is an English instructor at Navajo Community College in Tsaile, Arizona. Her previously published works include *The Sacred: Ways of Knowledge, Sources of Life; The Sun Is Not Merciful; The Spirit of Native America; Ghost Singer;* and *Talking Indian: Reflections on Writing and Survival.* This is her first children's book.

CAROL BOWLES is an artist who has been living in and exploring the Southwest for twelve years. She uses the richness and diversity of her New Mexican surroundings as the background for her paintings. Ms. Bowles lives in Santa Fe, where she is working on a series about the New Mexico pueblos.